THE FIRST PEOPLE

OF MARYLAND

HETTIE   BOYCE-BALLWEBER

1987
Maryland Historical Press
9205 Tuckerman Street
Lanham, MD 20706 USA

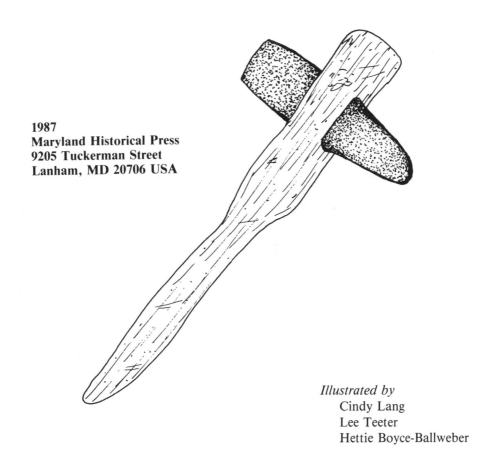

Illustrated by
Cindy Lang
Lee Teeter
Hettie Boyce-Ballweber

Copyright © 1987 Hettie Boyce-Ballweber

Published by Maryland Historical Press,
Lanham, Maryland 20706, USA
SAN 2026147
ISBN 0-917882-24-5

Library of Congress Catalog Card Number 8 7 - 0 6 1 0 6 6
Manufactured in the United States of America

Second Printing 1993
Third Printing   1999

ABOUT THE AUTHOR

Hettie Boyce-Ballweber has been a professional archaeologist for the past six years, having done most of her work in Pennsylvania and Maryland. She received her Bachelor of Arts degree, summa cum laude, majoring in anthropology, from California University of Pennsylvania, and is presently completing a Masters of Applied Anthropology from University of Maryland, College Park. She is the author of over 30 technical reports and four articles in professional journals.

As well as her involvement in archaeology, she has had over 12 years experience working in the Pennsylvania public schools and in volunteer parent-teacher associations where she has held such offices as regional vice president, state public relations chairman, president of local, council and regional units, and cultural arts chairman. She has also served on various ad hoc committees concerning school improvement plans, curriculum development, and has served on Pennsylvania's Reading Rainbow Program Committee.

Acknowledgements

Special thanks to the following people who contributed
in some way to the creation of this book:

Kate Ballweber — teacher
Erve Chambers — anthropologist
Lois Brown — archeologist
C. Laurie Clement — editor
Dennis Curry — archeologist
Joe Dent — archeologist

To my husband, Bill, whose computer expertise, creativity and
enthusiasm added a unique dimension to this book. This book is
also for my sons, Mike and Steve, who have contributed greatly
to my respect and admiration for children.

NOTE FROM THE AUTHOR FOR TEACHERS

People in the United States have been discovering, in the past 20 or 30 years, that they possess a rich heritage in which they can take pride. As a result, prehistoric and historic preservation projects and outdoor museums have been springing up all over the country. Millions of people each year spend their vacations visiting historical sites, archaeological investigations and museums. There has been unprecedented popularity in multi-episodal historical television dramas and historical novels. The enactment of Federal and State laws has been demonstrative of the public's interest in the Nation's cultural heritage.

The recent changes in the attitude of Americans toward a renewed sense of national heritage have been beneficial to the nation's overall image and sense of pride. However, there has not been an effective approach by archaeologists to provide youngsters with a concept of our cultural heritage, although archaeology can play a useful role in school curriculums in that it can make the study of history and social studies more attractive and useful to students. The archaeological record, which is abundant in Maryland, can expose students to the study of cultural evolution through a "reconstruction" of the past. The introduction of prehistoric culture in its proper sequence before the arrival of the colonists and their contact with Indians can enlighten the child's understanding of the processes involved with man's adaptation and changes in relationship to his environment.

Materials simply cannot teach themselves. However, a carefully thought out, appropriately created supplemental resource may be the catalyst in making the teaching of a particular subject both intriguing and fun, while meeting the goals and objectives of the curriculum.

In creating a useful supplement for the classroom, the following criteria was established:
1. It had to appeal to the student's interest and ability to comprehend.
2. It had to be useful to the teacher.
3. It had to meet the goals and objectives of the curriculum.

It is hoped that this book will provide a knowledge of archaeology and Maryland's prehistory while at the same time providing hours of reading enjoyment.

TABLE OF CONTENTS

INTRODUCTION

In 1634, colonists from England arrived in America to make a new home for themselves in what would become Maryland. Here, they met the Indians, people far different from themselves. The colonists, or "settlers," traded objects with the Indians, for food and land, things they had brought with them from Europe, like beads, tools and cloth. They traded for land on which to build their houses. Some colonists, like Captain John Smith and Father Andrew White, visited the Indians and wrote in diaries about how they lived. You probably have some ideas about what those Indians looked like because you have seen drawings or have read stories about how they lived in Maryland. What you already know about the Indians is from what has been written down in the past. This is called history. Maryland Indians had no written history. They did not write at all, except for carving pictures on large rocks or stones.

But, did you know that when the colonists arrived in Maryland the Indians had already been there for thousands of years? We know this because of the work that **archaeologists** do. You will learn in this booklet what happened in Maryland many thousands of years ago. What happened in the past before things were written down is called **prehistory.** (I bet you're not surprised!).

This booklet is divided into two parts. The first part will tell you something about how archaeologists go about their jobs of "digging" into the past. The second part will be a trip back in time to 10,000 years ago. Then you will move forward to the time when the settlers landed in Maryland. You are going to take a 10,000 year time trip! You can stop along the way for some games and activities to help make your trip a bit more fun.

PART I

LEARNING ABOUT ARCHAEOLOGY

LET'S GET STARTED!!
What Is Archaeology?

Archaeology is a science which studies prehistory. It is the study of how people lived in the past by looking at the things they left behind. An archaeologist can look at objects left behind by **prehistoric** peoples to determine how these people lived.

Although some archaeologists study parts of history, for our unit we will be talking about **prehistory,** or the time before things were written down.

You may think it would be very difficult to study something for which there is no written record. You are right! But archaeologists read a different kind of record. They read a record of **artifacts.** Artifacts are anything made by people. For studying prehistory, archaeologists look at the objects left behind by the people who made and used them. You make artifacts all the time. Every time you throw something in the trash can, you are throwing away an artifact. When you are outside with your friends your activities can create artifacts. When you were little, did you ever wonder how your parents knew what you had been doing by looking at where you left your toys? Now you know! An archaeologist can tell by looking at objects and where they were left, what people were doing.

All people make artifacts. Prehistoric people made artifacts out of stone, like spear points, axes, hammers

3

and bowls. These artifacts last for a long time. They also made things from bone, shells and wood. These objects do not last as long as stone objects. Do you know why? Because nature **preserves** things differently. Shell, bone, wooden objects and food decay easily. Archaeologists know this, and understand **preservation** when they look at artifacts.

One of the most important jobs an archaeologist has is studying many types of artifacts to understand how different groups lived. Some groups made different types of tools than others. Because of this, archaeologists can tell where different groups lived and sometimes even how long they lived there. A place where artifacts are found is called a **site.** (Don't get this word mixed up with the word "sight" meaning "to see.") A site is any place where people have lived or rested for a time, and left something behind. Sites can be very big, with lots of artifacts (like your room when it needs to be cleaned!) or very small with only a few artifacts. You will learn about different types of sites later during your "time travel."

WHAT DO ARCHAEOLOGISTS DO?

Archaeologists find sites, all over the world. It is one of their favorite jobs! It is also very important to study them. There are many, many sites in Maryland. You may even know where one is if you know anyone who has found arrowheads. Perhaps you have found some, too. Most of the time archaeologists know where to find sites because prehistoric people liked to live in certain places better than others. Can you guess where these places may be? Hint: Prehistoric people needed to be

close to food and water, just like you. They needed shelter, just like you, and they also needed to be close to the materials which they used to make their tools. Answer: Sites can be found next to streams, in caves, under rock overhangs, or on hilltops. They also would be close to where the animals roamed so people could hunt them. Try to think about what people needed in order to live. The streams and rivers provided water and fish for food. Caves and rock overhangs provided shelter from rain, wind and cold weather. Rocks and cobblestones from the rivers and streams were used for making tools.

Archaeologists look for sites in all these places. How do they find sites? That's a good question. They look in all the places where they think prehistoric people might have liked to live. They look in these places, and especially in the fields where farmers have plowed to plant seed.

Many times a plow will turn up artifacts that were under the surface of the ground. Sometimes archaeologists look inside caves, or along river banks.

When an archaeologist looks for sites, it is called a **survey.** Many times surveys are done before a new road or buildings are built so that sites will not be destroyed. It is very important to study these sites, for once they are destroyed, no one will ever learn anything about the people who were there. Sometimes sites are found by accident, by people building houses, by the farmer plowing his fields, or maybe even by you while you are playing outside with your friends.

How does an archaeologist study a site after he has found it? He does an **excavation** (maybe you call it "digging"). An excavation is a scientific way of digging a site. First, an archaeologist will look closely at the type of artifacts found on a site. If you were to visit an archaeological site, you might ask, "How do you know where to begin digging?" That's another good question! Well, after looking at the artifacts found in an area, the

archaeologist may not know enough about the site. So he may have to dig **test pits.** A test pit is a small hole dug with a shovel to find more artifacts. Usually the dirt or soil that is removed from the hole is carefully **screened.** Have you ever sifted sand in a sandbox or at the beach? Remember how small pebbles and shells were left behind because they were too big to pass through the screen? When the dirt from a test pit passes through the screen, the artifacts are left behind.

The archaeologist uses the screen to save *all* the artifacts so the site can be "read" by the artifacts. Test pits help the archaeologist tell where a site begins and ends. When no more artifacts are found in the test pits, you are no longer on the site.

Many times the archaeologist wants to save a site. In fact, today, most sites are studied because they would otherwise be destroyed. Archaeologists **excavate** sites in different ways. One way is to do the work by using shovels and hoes. When large areas are to be excavated, sometimes machines such as bulldozers are used to clear the ground. Once the archaeologist knows where the site is, he will make a map of the site using special tools. The site is usually divided up into large squares, called "units," and there are special numbers given to each one. Wooden stakes are pounded into the ground at the corners of the squares, and string is tied to them, dividing up the units. When this is done, a site can look like a giant checkerboard. This is called a **grid.** Why is this done? So every artifact can be given its very own special location.

Remember the farmer who plowed his field and turned up some prehistoric artifacts? Well, suppose that we are going to excavate the site he found in his field. Many of the sites in Maryland that have been excavated have been started in just this way. When the farmer plowed the soil, the layer of dirt that was all mixed up by the plow is called the **plowzone.** It is a darker color and will be removed when the site is excavated, but all the artifacts mixed up by the plow will be kept. They can still be studied for the way they are made, or for how old they are.

What the archaeologist really wants to see is what the plow hasn't mixed up! Beneath the plowzone is another type of soil called **subsoil,** which means the soil under the topsoil (I bet you weren't surprised). This subsoil is lighter in color because roots of plants do not reach it to make it darker and richer. The subsoil is the best place to look for prehistoric activity, much like your parents look under your bed to see the real you! It is also called undisturbed soil because no one has touched it (except maybe prehistoric people who lived there). Now, so far we have already learned that the archaeologist studies **artifacts,** or those things made by people. However archaeologists do not always study just artifacts. Prehistoric people also left other signs of living or camping somewhere, and archaeologists really want to know about that.

Indians dug holes. Because they had not yet learned

about building homes with stoves or refrigerators, the Indians had to do other things to survive. They dug holes to make fire pits for cooking, or keeping warm. They dug other holes to store food in, and some other holes were for throwing garbage away. Some were used to set posts made from young trees to build houses, and some holes were dug to bury their dead.

All of these holes were later filled in. The soil that went back into them was usually darker topsoil, along with trash sometimes. Imagine yourself digging a hole.

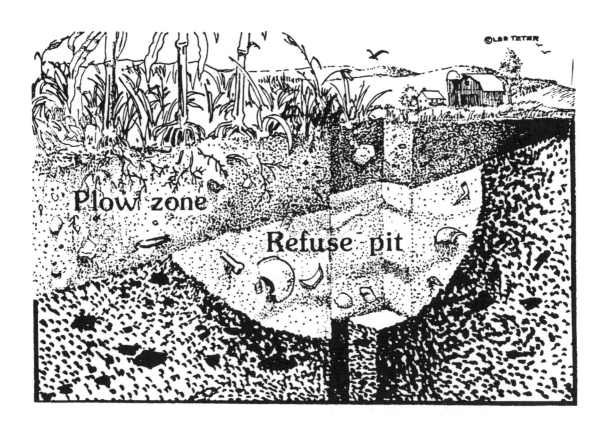

You throw the dirt off to the side. But when you fill the hole back up, do you put the dirt back in exactly as you took it out? That would be impossible. When this mixed-up soil fills in the hole, it makes the soil in the hole darker than before. An archaeologist can see these differences. He even has a name for it. It is called a **feature.**

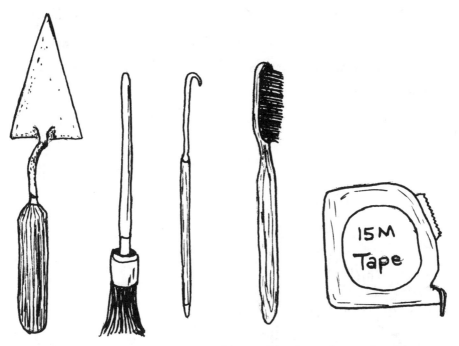

Archaeologists use various kinds of tools for excavating. Many of these tools are bought in the hardware store. The typical tool of the archaeologist is a mason's trowel. Other "tools" include dental tools, tape measures, dust pans, whisk brooms, string and small brushes. Archaeologists are very careful with their tools, and take special care to keep them clean and in good condition.

So when an archaeologist excavates a site, he (or she!) removes the topsoil or plowzone, and looks for the features in the subsoil (Whew!). What they are really looking at are the Indian-dug holes which have been filled in over hundreds of years of time. By later drawing the features on maps (remember the large unit grid or "checkerboard" map?), archaeologists can see where the fire pits were, and where the trash pits were too. They can also see where the houses were by looking at features called **postmolds,** which are dark spots left in the soil where posts used to be.

postmolds

Archaeologists then slowly dig out the soil in the features. The soil is then screened to collect all the artifacts. The artifacts will be studied carefully later in a laboratory.

Many other important things that are done when excavating a site take much time. But it is very important not to forget anything. Archaeologists take careful **field notes.** These field notes will tell others what has been found and where it was found at the site as well as how the site was excavated.

Photographs of all the features and sometimes of the artifacts are part of the field notes.

When the excavation is complete, the archaeologist puts all the dirt back over the site so it looks the way he found it. Then he returns to the laboratory where all the artifacts, field notes and maps are studied. The artifacts are carefully washed and labeled with numbers, telling where they came from in the units. Now comes the hard part! The archaeologist must "read" the artifacts and features since written words are not available. The labelled

A numbered artifact

artifacts are described, drawn, and sometimes photographed. They are then separated into different categories such as bone, stone, pottery or shell. People who are specially trained look at the bone to tell what types of animals were hunted or eaten. Nutshells and small seeds are studied to tell what kinds of plants were grown or collected for food. Sometimes stone tools and pottery are compared with those found on other excavated sites to see if they look the same. By doing this, archaeologists can tell how people lived at a site or if they had contact with people from other sites nearby or far away. This job is called **interpreting** a site. You have just learned what archaeologists do to learn about prehistoric peoples.

There are many other things archaeologists do too. Some of these are hard to do without your help. You can help report and protect archaeological sites. Every day, sites in Maryland are destroyed, most of the time in the process of building new roads, putting in gas pipelines, sewer lines, or electric power lines. But sometimes sites in the way of this building are excavated by archaeologists before they get destroyed. That is because these sites are protected by laws. The President has signed many bills to save sites from destruction. Some sites are *not* protected though. Also, many people steal artifacts or dig holes at sites without permission. This stops the archaeologist from reading those sites because they need to see all the artifacts from a site to tell how people lived there.

If you find a site or know someone who has, you should report it to the Maryland State Archaeologist's office. At this office, many trained people keep track of the sites found in Maryland. There are over 6000 sites now recorded. This means that much can be told about Maryland's first people. Without people who know how archaeologists work, and who report artifacts, we may never know about the ancestors of the Indians who met the first settlers in Maryland.

ACTIVITIES
ABOUT PRESERVATION

1. Make a menu for the following meals: (1) a typical dinner in your home, (2) a meal at a fast-food hamburger restaurant, and (3) a lunch at a school cafeteria. Make a list of the foods from those meals that would survive outside, under normal conditions, until the year 5000.

2. After you have made your list, think about what would remain (containers, cooking utensils, etc.) that would tell you about the food we eat. Remember that metal, ceramics, plastics and glass survive a long time, but that paper doesn't.

3. Discuss what this activity teaches about archaeological sites. Do archaeologists get a good idea of what people ate? Can archaeologists ever be sure of all the foods people ate at any archaeological site? Discuss other types of remains that may not be completely preserved at an archaeological site. What about clothing and tools (made of wood, fiber or bone), that might have been used 1,000 years ago? Would archaeologists find evidence of all of these? When an archaeologist excavates a site that is 5,000 or 10,000 years old and only finds stone points, what does this mean? Do you think the archaeologist is limited in what can be known about people because of preservation?

ARTIFACTS OF AMERICA

1. List 10 artifacts to put into a time capsule that would represent American life. What would these artifacts tell about our life?

2. Write down the reason you chose each artifact, and try to guess what the archaeologist who digs them up might say about them. Do any of the artifacts present different ideas?

3. Draw a picture below of your time capsule. Where would you bury it? Why do you think that would be a good place? Would it be safe there for a long time? (Think about new roads, homes, and shopping centers which are being built all around us.)

VOCABULARY

Archaeology   The scientific study of the remains of past human life

Artifact   An object people have made or modified

Excavation   The study of an archaeological site by carefully digging the layers of earth

Feature   Cultural remains (more than a single artifact) such as house floors, storage pits, firehearths, burials, or cooking pits

Field notes   Information written down by the archaeologist while in the field to aid in the interpretation of the site

Grid   A graph of uniformly spaced lines that divides a site into equal size squares

Interpret   To understand the meaning

Postmold   A dark circular stain left in the ground after a post decays

Prehistoric Archaeology	The study of archaeological sites which existed before the settlers arrived in Maryland
Preservation	To keep from rotting or destruction; protection
Screening	The process of sifting excavated soil through fine wire screen in order to catch small artifacts
Site	Any place that has remains of past human activity
Subsoil	The undisturbed soil underneath the topsoil
Survey	Carefully looking over an area to find archaeological sites
Test pit	A pit that is excavated on an archaeological site to determine the importance of buried remains

THE PICNIC

Suppose you attended a big picnic after school with your friends. When you got there, you saw many people you know, and there were a lot of good things to eat. Now, suppose someone forgot to bring the garbage cans! So everyone just dropped their trash on the ground around the picnic tables. What a mess!

After many rainy and sunny days, if someone visited the place where you had your picnic, what would they be able to tell about what you and your friends did?

On a piece of paper make a list from one to five: What things would still be there for someone to see? What would have decayed and would no longer be there? What would those things tell about you and your friends?

Now, compare your list with some of your friends who also made a list. Did you all think of the same things? What was the same? What was different?

THINGS TO DO WITH YOUR
FRIENDS OR FAMILY

1. Visit an archaeological dig and ask the archaeologists to explain how they are excavating the site and what they think has happened at it.

2. Report an archaeological site to the State Archaeologist. Do you have a friend or relative who has collected artifacts, or have you? If so, you may ask where the artifacts came from and then let someone at the State Archaeologist's office know where the site is (of course with the permission of your friend or relative).

> State Archaeologist
> Maryland Geological Survey
> Division of Archaeology
> 2300 St. Paul Street
> Baltimore, Maryland 21218

3. Attend a local archaeological society meeting. There may be one close to where you live. They are listed in the back of this booklet.

4. Visit museums that have archaeological displays. Can you tell by looking at the artifacts how they were used?

5. Suppose you had to move away from your house suddenly and leave everything. Discuss with your family: In 300 years, what would be left for an archaeologist to find? How would the weather have affected what was left? What would untrained collectors and looters have taken? (Most of the valuables!) Do you think the archaeologist could tell anything about you and your family?

WORD GAME

Circle the correct answer.

1. Archaeologists "read" prehistoric sites by looking at the:
    A. Indian's diary
    B. Road map
    C. Artifacts and features
    D. Rocks

2. Prehistoric man liked to live close to:
    A. Food and water
    B. Fast food restaurants
    C. Golf courses
    D. Home

3. The time before things were written down is called:
    A. History
    B. Prehistory
    C. Confusing
    D. Unknown

4. Archaeologists study an archaeological site by carefully digging layers of earth. This is called:
    A. Science
    B. Work
    C. Mapping
    D. Excavation

5. Any object that people have made or modified is called an:
    A. Oracle
    B. Artifact
    C. Artichoke
    D. Tent pole

6. The scientific study of the remains of past human life is done by:
   A. Magicians
   B. Chemists
   C. Archaeologists
   D. Musicians

7. When archaeologists divide a site into equal sized squares for excavation, it is then called a:
   A. DigCheck
   B. Checkerboard
   C. Grid
   D. Mess

8. When Indians dug holes for storage, burials, fire pits and post holes, archaeologists find them later and call them:
   A. Stonebins
   B. Cradlemounds
   C. Features
   D. Ropeyarns

9. When archaeologists sift soil to gather artifacts, this is called:
   A. Digging
   B. Screening
   C. Mapping
   D. Designing

10. When archaeologists dig small holes to find out where a site is and to decide how important the artifacts are, these holes are called:
    A. Fire pits
    B. Snakey pits
    C. Test pits
    D. Arm pits

11. Any place that has remains of past human activity is called a:
    A. Cave dig
    B. Post hole
    C. Site
    D. Jammin' stance

12. When an archaeologist writes down all the facts about an excavation into a notebook, they are called:
    A. Fairy tales
    B. Dissertation
    C. Field notes
    D. Journals

13. When an archaeologist talks about what prehistoric people were doing on a site, this is called:
    A. Mind reading
    B. Interpretation
    C. Interlogging
    D. Interstellar navigation

WORD FIND

Find the following word in the diagram below, and draw a line in the crossword for each word that you find.

archaeologist	grid	trowel
shovel	field notes	features
survey	interpret	test pit
screening	map	prehistory
excavation	postmold	artifact
plowzone	preservation	subsoil
site		

```
U  F  A  T  S  E  O  P  T  R  M  O  I  N
A  R  T  I  F  A  C  T  P  Z  A  O  N  Y
R  Z  U  B  P  S  T  G  R  I  D  C  T  Z
C  E  A  R  S  U  R  V  E  Y  T  D  E  M
H  I  M  H  N  B  O  E  H  S  W  M  R  O
A  P  A  T  E  S  T  P  I  T  X  L  P  P
E  D  P  C  A  O  F  J  S  I  T  E  R  O
O  E  L  R  Z  I  K  G  T  H  J  F  E  S
L  Z  F  I  E  L  D  N  O  T  E  S  T  T
O  R  H  M  B  S  X  T  R  O  W  E  L  M
G  D  W  C  B  P  E  Q  Y  O  K  C  V  O
I  S  O  G  E  Z  Y  R  U  E  A  N  B  L
S  H  O  V  E  L  A  S  V  T  X  A  F  D
T  H  J  A  L  O  Q  F  E  A  T  U  R  E
P  L  O  W  Z  O  N  E  I  O  T  H  D  K
S  G  Y  V  L  S  C  R  E  E  N  I  N  G
W  X  J  P  E  X  C  A  V  A  T  I  O  N
Q  M  X  V  B  L  R  P  G  L  I  B  E  N
```

PART II

LET'S TAKE A TRIP THROUGH TIME

TIME TRAVEL

Try, if you can, to imagine what it would be like to travel back in time to over 10,000 years ago. Of course, that would be very difficult! No one has been able to physically travel to that period in time to see what it was really like. Archaeologists have been able to "read" what it might have been like for the people who lived during that time by studying the artifacts they left behind. Of course, archaeologists have been helped by **geologists.** Geologists study the different ages of rocks and look at the changes that take place in rivers and land over time.

It may be helpful to remember before we start our time trip that Maryland has changed very much since the first people arrived. As these changes took place, people learned to **adapt** to their natural surroundings. **Adaptation** means that we learn to adjust to the changes taking place around us. We turn the furnace on when winter comes and we put on our warm coats and socks. The early people of Maryland also made the same type of adjustments. However, those adjustments were made slowly. Today things are constantly changing. But we don't always see those changes because they take a very long time to happen. Do you remember when you were two years old? You may not, but your mother can tell you that you have changed a lot since then. Sometimes we adjust without even knowing it. This is what happened to the people who lived in Maryland.

We also need to remember before we begin that the early people of Maryland were greatly **influenced** by their natural surroundings. This means that things like weather and availability of water and food made a difference in where they lived and how well they got along. So when we stop on our trip through time to talk about the prehistoric people living then, remember that they adapted to conditions at that time the best they knew how.

Another thing we need to learn is how archaeologists measure time. All time is measured before and after the time of Christ. You know that we are living approximately 2000 years after the birth of Christ. This time is written as **A.D.** The time before Christ was born is written as **B.C.** It might be better if you saw a diagram of this to understand it.

```
I ----------------------------- I ----------------------------- I
2,000 B.C.           The birth              A.D. 1986
                     of Christ
```

So as you go back in time before Christ, you should remember that if we are talking of 1,000 B.C., we really mean 2986 years ago! (1986 + 1000 = 2986)

The key words to remember on our time travel are:

environment   influence   adaptation

The prehistoric people were influenced by their environment. They adapted to these influences.

THE
PALEO-INDIAN

The first people reached Maryland between 11,000 to 9,000 B.C. Archaeologists aren't sure exactly when they got to Maryland because so few of their artifacts are left. In fact, only those things which didn't decay are left. Something you may be asking now is "Where did they come from?" Good question! Archaeologists think that the earliest Americans came to North America (the United States and Canada) as long ago as 18,000 years! Why did they come and from where? Well imagine this: Around 18,000 years ago part of the United States was covered by a large sheet of ice. This sheet of ice, called a **glacier,** produced an "ice age." The glacier was called the Wisconsin Glacier. If you are thinking that it had to be cold, you are right! The water for this ice sheet came from the Atlantic and Pacific Oceans.

Now, because a lot of the water from both oceans was frozen in the glacier, the shorelines of the United States were very different from those we see today. When we go to the beach today, a lot of the area now covered by water was land during the ice age. In the North-western part of the United States where the Arctic Ocean is now, a bridge of land was formed that con-

nected Siberia with Alaska. This land bridge is called
Beringia.

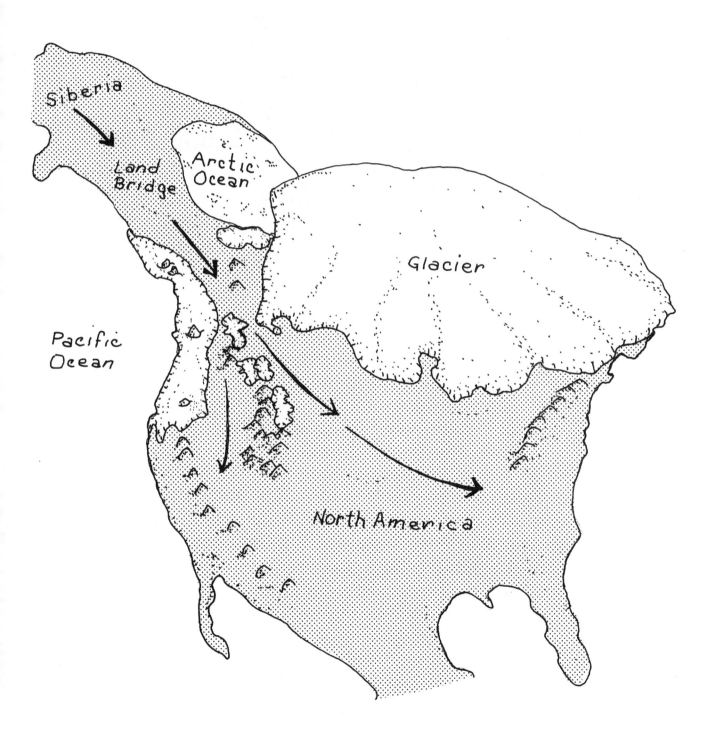

Wild grasses, mosses and small shrubs grew on this land bridge making it a **tundra.**

This tundra provided food for animals to graze. Animals were different then too. These animals were adapted to the colder weather and tundra vegetation. They roamed the grassland eating as they went. What kinds of animals were they? They were mostly large animals that lived in **herds**—like the wooly mammoth, caribou, musk-ox and mastodon. The people living in Siberia followed the animals across Beringia hunting them for food. These people spread out over America until they eventually reached Maryland.

Archaeologists called these people **Paleo-Indians. Paleo** means **ancient,** so these people really are called the ancient Indians.

Remember, the Paleo-Indian did not cross America in a few days. It may have taken 7,000 YEARS to reach Maryland. So the first Paleo-Indians that came to America were not the same ones that reached Maryland.

As time went by, the glacier melted a little. As this happened, the oceans rose higher and the land bridge became covered with water. Today the land bridge is completely under water. Siberia and Alaska are now separated by the Arctic Ocean. The glacier also was making changes in Maryland that we shall soon see.

Maryland looked much like the tundra of Beringia because the edge of the glacier was very close. The animals that were hunted were the same type of herd animals as lived in Beringia. The Paleo-Indian surrounded the animal and threw many spears at it until they killed it. Then they sliced up the meat and took it back to their camps.

The Paleo-Indian was a master at making tools. The best known Paleo-Indian artifact is the **fluted spear-point.**

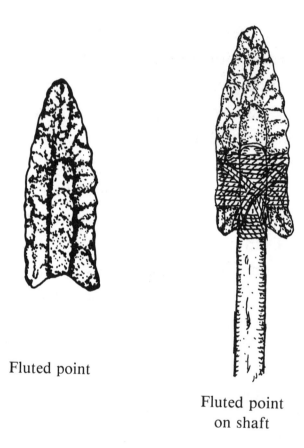

Fluted point

Fluted point
on shaft

The spearpoints that have been found in Maryland are very beautiful and finely made. The spearpoints were made from chipping and shaping very hard stone called **chert.** This chert was found all over Maryland and in other states. Much of the chert used to make the spearpoints was from other states. Spearpoints were made by striking a block of chert with another stone. This stone is called a **hammerstone.** It broke **flakes** from the chert which would then be shaped into a spearpoint.

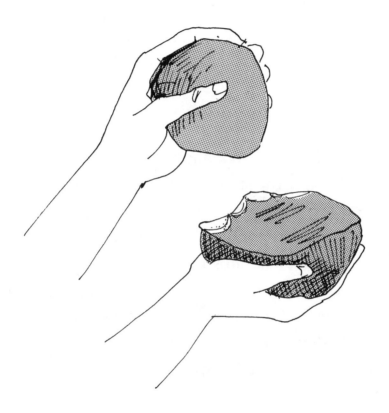

A **flute** was notched into the point so it could be tied onto a wooden spear. Some of these flakes were made into **knives,** for cutting meat and grains, and **scrapers** for removing hides for clothing.

Knife   Scraper

These tools were also made from chert. The word archaeologists use for stone is **lithic** which means stone. So if you see lithic tools written about in a book, you will know they are tools made from stone.

The Paleo-Indians mostly hunted animals for food. But they also gathered wild berries, seeds, nuts, roots, and bird's eggs. Since preservation over 10,000 years is not good, the only artifacts that have been found in Maryland are the fluted spearpoints, knives, scrapers and hammerstones.

Archaeologists know where Paleo-Indians liked to stay. Paleo-Indian artifacts have been found in caves and rockshelters. They camped for short periods of times near streams. If their camps were outside of rockshelters and caves, they usually were near water and where the sun would shine on them for warmth. They hunted the animals that roamed nearby and caught fish in the streams and rivers.

Hunting the Mastodon

Remember how we talked about how the climate must have been cool because of the glacier? Well, the Paleo-Indian probably had to wear the right kind of clothing to keep warm. Their clothing was made out of animals hides. They may have built shelters using small young trees called saplings. Over a shell of these saplings which they set into the ground, they threw animal hides. These shelters probably looked a lot like small tents. Paleo-Indians did not live in one place too long because they had to follow the animals. If plants were not available during some seasons of the year, they had to move to a place where they could look for food.

Archaeologists think the life of the Paleo-Indian was a hard life. But the Paleo-Indians did not know that. They cooperated with nature the best they could. As time went by they grew in numbers and learned new ways of adapting to the changes taking place around them.

VOCABULARY

Adaptation   The process of changing to fit into a situation.

A.D.   What archaeologists use for talking about a date after the birth of Christ.

Beringia   The "ice age" land bridge that connected Alaska with Siberia.

B.C.   What archaeologists use for talking about a date before the birth of Christ.

Environment   All the conditions under which any one or thing lives.

Chert   A very hard stone which "flakes" when it is hit hard. It was used by prehistoric people to make tools.

Flute   A groove chipped into a spearpoint to allow it to be tied onto a spear.

Glacier   A large sheet of ice that creates an "ice age."

Geologist   A person who studies the history of the earth as recorded in rocks.

Herd   A group of animals that live and roam together.

Tundra   A treeless plain covered with mosses, wild grasses and shrubs.

VOCABULARY ACTIVITIES

Can you match the following words?

Paleo	Adjust
B.C.	Spearpoint
Adapt	Shelter
Beringia	Grassland
Cave	Before Christ
Tundra	Ancient
A.D.	Land Bridge
Fluted	After Christ

SCRAMBLED WORDS

dfutel rpostapeni	_____ _____
adnl rbiegde	_____ _____
ahsmetomrn	_____
aciburo	_____
srkhetlocer	_____
fekla	_____
tafricta	_____
gicelar	_____

ACTIVITIES
THINK AND DO

1. If you were a Paleo-Indian, what would be the most important tools that you would take with you when you travelled? If you had to leave something behind, what would it be? Write your answers on a sheet of paper and compare them with your friends. Talk about your answers.

2. Draw a picture of what you think a Paleo-Indian camp would look like in winter.

3. If you were a Paleo-Indian, how far would you be willing to walk for water? Where would you look for animals to hunt? Why?

4. Write a short story about a Paleo-Indian boy going on his first hunt with his father. Describe what he would see and do during the hunt. What do you suppose his sister was doing while he was hunting?

MAP ACTIVITY

Look at the following map of Maryland. The dots show where fluted spearpoints have been found. Can you guess why the points were found in those places? Write your answer below the map in a short sentence.

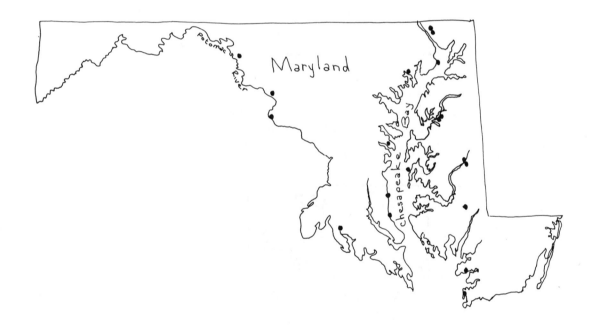

Chesapeake Bay

Before

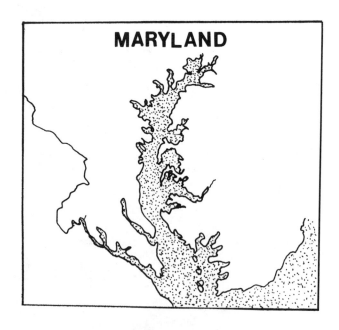

After

48

THE ARCHAIC HUNTERS
AND GATHERERS

As we visited the Paleo-Indians, changes in the environment were taking place. The climate was gradually changing, but as we remember, the changes were so slow that the Paleo-Indian did not notice it. Remember that these changes took several thousand years!

As you imagine how the Paleo-Indians lived, continue to imagine that the climate begins to warm a little. We are now standing at a time that will last almost 7000 years! That's a lot of birthdays ago!!! This time is called the **Archaic** period (8,000 B.C. to 1,000 B.C.). It has been given this name by archaeologists because the changes that took place during the Paleo-Indian time led to a slight change in how people lived.

The biggest change that took place during the Archaic period was in the Wisconsin glacier. It slowly began to melt. As it melted, it moved farther and farther away from Maryland. Can you guess what else began to happen? Remember how Beringia became covered with water? That also happened to parts of Maryland. As the ice melted, water from the glacier started to fill up the cracks and low spots in the ground. All this water eventually formed the Chesapeake Bay. Remember that before this, the Chesapeake Bay was land that the prehistoric people lived on and walked across as they hunted.

The glacier melted as the climate slowly warmed. Those large animals that were adapted to the cooler climate followed the glacier. The tundra also changed. Trees started growing as it got warmer. Soon Maryland was covered with forests. Animals who were adapted to the forests were smaller, and became plentiful. As these changes took place, Maryland slowly began to look much like it does today. You would even be able to recognize Maryland as it looked then. Some of the animals that roamed the forests then were rabbits, squirrels, wolves, bison, porcupines, beavers and white-tailed deer.

These smaller animals could not be hunted with the large fluted spearpoints that the hunters had been able to use successfully before. So the Archaic hunters used a different technology to make spearpoints. (**Technology** is the way people make something.) Instead, the Archaic people made smaller spearpoints than their ancestors, the Paleo-Indians.

The new spearpoints were

stemmed   and notched.

Points were no longer fluted. This is because the spear the Archaic hunters used was different from what the Paleo-Indian used. (Archaeologists call spearpoints and arrowheads "projectile points." **Projectile** means anything that is "projected" or is thrown through the air.)

The best known artifact from the Archaic period is called the **atlatl** (pronounced at lattle), or spear thrower. Attached to the spearthrower was a stone, sometimes polished, called a **bannerstone.** This was used as a weight to help the spear travel with greater force. It helped the hunter toss the spear further and faster.

Remember, spears were all that were used to hunt the animals that ran fast, like the deer. Have you ever tried to run after a rabbit? They are fast, aren't they? The

Archaic hunter was very smart to invent the atlatl!

They also added other things to their tool kits. They ground stones by hand, rubbing other stones against them like sandpaper to make them smooth. These ground stones were shaped into axes, adzes, gouges, tools for woodworking.

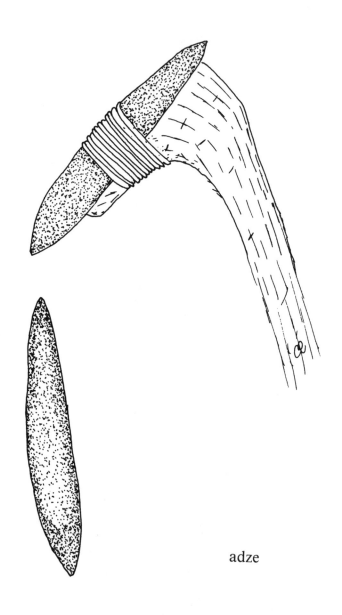

adze

Besides spearpoints and woodworking tools, other important tools used were scrapers, drills and knives. Remember how the Paleo-Indian used chert to make his fluted spearpoints? Well, the Archaic hunters and gatherers used other types of

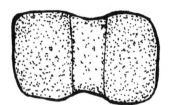

axe

stone, or chert, found in Maryland. It was no longer brought in from other states.

Drill and use of drill

What was happening during this time? The Archaic hunters and gatherers learned how to use what nature provided to their advantage. They hunted the wild animals in the forests. They gathered all the wild plants and seeds around them, and they fished from the streams and rivers. Their eating habits changed over time. They also gathered oysters and other shellfish from the Chesapeake Bay, rivers and streams. Can you picture the Archaic hunters and gatherers at their first bull and oyster roast, or blue crab feast?

Archaeologists know that Archaic people ate oysters and clams from the Chesapeake Bay because large piles of shells, called **middens,** are found along the shores of the Bay. These are places where the shells would be thrown after the meal (like you throw your leftovers in the trash can!). Archaic spearpoints have been found in these shell middens, because they were thrown away (into the Archaic "trash can") or accidentally lost while the shells were being tossed away. Sometimes these shell middens contain thousands and thousands of shells, and archaeologists sometimes have to work very hard to find important artifacts, like spearpoints, among the mounds of oyster shells.

There are many Archaic sites in Maryland. Mostly, what archaeologists find at these sites are spearpoints and ground stone tools. Most of the bone, shell and wooden objects have decayed away. (Remember when we talked about preservation?)

The Archaic Indians liked to live in the same places where the Paleo-Indians lived. They lived under rock overhangs, in caves, on hilltops overlooking streams, or where two streams joined. They liked to camp in spots where the sun would shine the longest or brightest.

The Archaic people lived in groups like the Paleo-Indian, but as time went by, they lived so well with nature that they grew in numbers. They lived in small family groups called **bands.** (Think of a neighborhood of five or six houses.) As the seasons changed, they moved to gather berries, seeds, plants, and they hunted the animals, fished and gathered shellfish. They cooked their food over fire. Their houses looked a lot like those of the Paleo-Indian. They stayed in one place a longer

58

time than the Paleo-Indians. Their houses were probably round or rectangular. Animal skins, grass and tree bark were probably used to cover saplings set into the ground. Houses were probably built where rockshelters or caves were not available. They would return to the same places over and over again. They knew where the animals would go in the fall and where the berries and tender wild vegetables and fruits would be in the summer.

Life for the Archaic people was still not easy. They had to make do with what nature provided for them. But they knew their natural surroundings very well and how to make the most from what was available to them. They became skillful hunters. Near the end of the Ar-

chaic period, they learned how to become even better at finding food. They used **fishwiers** to catch many fish at one time. A fishwier is a trap made from wood or stones. They were built in the rivers and streams. (Very clever!)

Fishwier
in the river

They also began grinding their food. Archaeologists know this because grinding stones have been found on Archaic sites. They are called

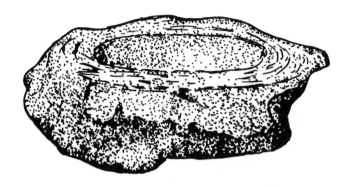

mortars

and

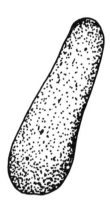

pestles.

The mortar serves as a bowl and the pestle is used to crush the food. There are also stone bowls found. These are usually carved out of **soapstone,** a soft, soapy-feeling stone that is easy to carve. It is also called **steatite.** This material comes from around the Chesapeake Bay. (Would you be surprised to find out that a lot of these bowls have been found there?)

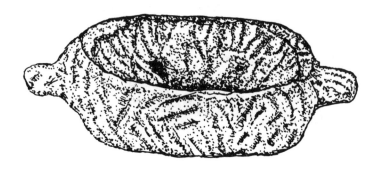

Have you enjoyed your visit with the Archaic hunters and gatherers? Try some of the activities before you go on to the next stop.

VOCABULARY

Atlatl   A spearthrower attached to the end of a spear, used for speed and accuracy.

Archaic   A name given by archaeologists to represent a period of time from 8000 B.C. to 1000 B.C.

Band   A small group of people who live and travel together.

Bannerstone   A spearthrower weight, used to make the spear travel faster.

Fishwier   A trap made of wood or stone to catch many fish.

Midden   A deposit or place where garbage was dumped.

Mortar   A slab or bowl used to hold seeds, grains or nuts for grinding.

Pestle   A stone used to grind seeds, grains or nuts.

Steatite   A soft, soapy-feeling stone that is easily carved.

Technology   The process of creating something—all the thoughts and actions that go into making something.

Tool kit   All the objects that people use for doing things in their daily lives.

ACTIVITIES

Here's a Scrabble-type game to try:

With your friends, make a list of words that describe the Archaic hunters and gatherers. The first person starts by printing a word on paper, like this:

G
A
T
H
E
R
E
R

The next person adds another word using one of the letters in the first word, like this:

G
ARCHAIC
T
H
E
R
E
R

As each person writes a word, explain the meaning of the word.

Suggestion: You may want to use your Scrabble game board and an unlimited number of letters for each player for this game.

ACTIVITIES

Mural Painting: With your family or friends draw a mural of an Archaic scene. You should use a large piece of paper, like from rolls of newsprint or butcher's paper. You can get this for free at many places if you ask. Think of all the things that Archaic hunters and gatherers would be doing. Use crayons, magic markers or waterpaints for your scene. Be sure to remember where Archaic sites would be found, and put the background scenery in as well.

Library Research Project: Visit your local library and look for books on archaeology. Look in the part of the books that talk about the Archaic period. Were the Archaic hunters and gatherers in other places different than those who lived in Maryland? In what ways were they different? In what ways were they the same?

Tool Making: Try striking two rocks together to break off small pieces. Look at the pieces and see if any look like they would make a good spearpoint. Can you imagine how long it would take to make a spearpoint? You may want to have an adult present when you do this project. (Be careful that you don't get pieces near your eyes.)

THE WOODLAND FARMERS

Things begin to change rapidly in our trip through time. As we left the Archaic hunters and gatherers, we saw that they were doing well in their natural surroundings. And we saw that other things were beginning to happen. As families grew, people did not move around as much. They became more settled. Now we go into a time period where changes took place over 2500 years! That's very fast when we realize that it took the Archaic period 7000 years to change! This period from 1000 B.C. to A.D. 1600 is called the **Woodland period.** The Indian lifestyle changed so much that the Woodland period can be divided into three periods: Early Woodland, Middle Woodland and Late Woodland.

So off we go again. You have learned how the natural environment of Maryland changed over a long time. Now it will be easier to imagine the Woodland period because it looked much like Maryland today. But, remember, there were no paved roads, no shopping malls, no houses, no fast food restaurants, and no skyscrapers! Picture in your mind that you are standing on a hilltop, looking out over woods, rivers and other hilltops. Streams are winding and flowing gently over rocks.

Then imagine that you are standing on the bank of a large river where you see fish jumping to catch flies and mosquitos. Imagine that you are standing along a beach on the Chesapeake Bay or the Atlantic Ocean. In all of these pictures, you would only see brush, trees, animals or water. There would be nothing else. That's what Maryland was like during Woodland times. If you have ever gone camping or walked in the woods, you know what it looked like.

Just as the Late Archaic hunters and gatherers learned to trap fish in the rivers and make bowls from stone, the Woodland farmers did that and even made them better.

Early Woodland People

During the Early Woodland period, people learned

how to make pottery. They learned that if they used clay from the ground and added different things like crushed rocks or shell, and placed it in the fire, it would come out as a finished pot for storing or cooking food. The rock and shell that was ground up and placed in the clay was called **temper.** The temper helped the clay stick together, sort of like prehistoric glue! The early pottery was made with slabs of clay, and shaped into posts which had flat bottoms with straight sides. Small lumps of clay added to the rims of the pots, called **lugs,** were used as handles. These pots were usually thick and heavy.

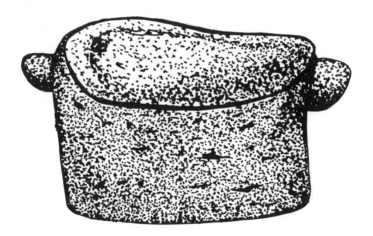

Later in the Woodland period, they made the pots and bowls by rolling clay in long strips and laying coils around and around on top of each other. It would soon look like a bowl or a pot, with a pointed bag shape. Then they gently smacked the soft clay all over with a

wooden paddle wrapped with a cord to help make the coils stick together. It also made **cordmarks** all over the pot.

In Maryland, archaeologists have found many sherds from the Early Woodland period. A **sherd** is a piece of a pot. If you dropped a dinner plate or bowl on the floor while you were drying dishes, it would probably break into pieces. These pieces are called sherds, but of course they would be modern day sherds. The sherds found on Early Woodland sites were not dropped and broken (at least not most of them); they were probably broken as they crumbled apart during the years because the early pottery did not preserve as well as stone. Archaeologists have found many whole pots in features that have been undisturbed. That's why we know how they were shaped. Also, many pots have been glued back together in laboratories from the sherds found after excavations. This was like putting together a three-dimensional jigsaw puzzle!!! The reassembled pots tell us what original pots looked like. We can also tell what temper the Indians used by looking at sherds. Some of the Early Woodland pottery was tempered with steatite or soap-stone, the same material that the Late Archaic hunters and gatherers carved into bowls. The Early Woodland people crushed the steatite for tempering.

Other changes were taking place on Early Woodland sites. People were learning to grow plants. They found out that the seeds they ate could be planted and, if given the proper care, would grow to provide even more food. Archaeologists think that **horticulture** began at this time. Archaeologists use the word horticulture to describe the way the Early Woodland people planted their seeds. It was much different than the way we plant a garden because the Early Woodland people were just beginners at "farming."

Even the tool kit of the Early Woodland people was different than Paleo-Indians and Late Archaic peoples. No longer was the atlatl used. Instead, small **corner-notched** and **side-notched** projectile points (arrowheads, spearheads) were used on wooden spear shafts.

notch ▶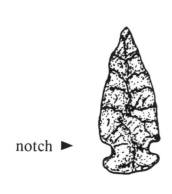

Another new pasttime was discovered: smoking. Some pipes found made from stone or clay tell archaeologists that smoking was important in some places in Maryland.

a pipe

A group from the Ohio area, called the Adena people, visited Maryland for a while. With them, they brought some ground stone tools, (can you remember the types of ground stone tools that we covered earlier?) and copper **beads,** and **pendants** made from stone, called **gorgets.**

Adena point

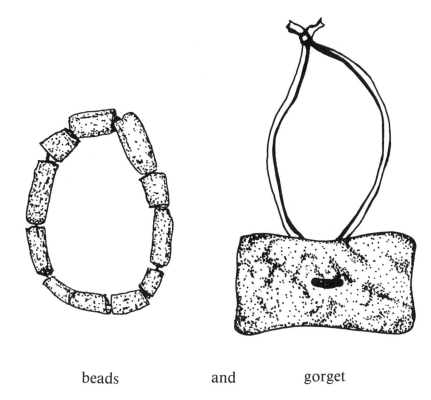

beads   and   gorget

The Adena were also different in that they buried their dead in large mounds of dirt, rather than holes in the ground. Archaeologists believe that they did not stay too long, because their artifacts have been found in just a few places in Maryland.

The Early Woodland people lived in larger groups or bands than the Archaic hunters and gatherers. During certain times of the year, these bands would gather together to collect the foods which were plentiful, usually in the late summer or fall. The plants, berries and nuts were all collected and eaten then, or saved for winter. By collecting a plentiful supply of food together so it wouldn't spoil, the Early Woodland people demonstrated that they could cooperate with their neighbors.

As in the Archaic period, people gathered together to collect oysters when they were plentiful, and dumped the shells into large piles along the river bank. Archaeologists have determined that there are many Woodland period shell middens along the Chesapeake Bay, too.

Hunting was also important, and favorite animals to eat were deer, rabbits, squirrels, turtles and birds of all kinds, including ducks, geese, turkeys and dove.

Their houses were located in the same types of places as Paleo-Indians and Archaic hunters and gatherers. They looked much the same as those before, with animal skins and bark covering small tree poles formed into huts. Some of the stones they used to make their tools were traded into Maryland from as far away as Ohio! But a lot of other stones were used that were found in different parts of Maryland.

Middle Woodland People

The changes that were taking place more quickly lead us into the Middle Woodland period. The reason archaeologists decided that a Middle Woodland period should be named is because pottery changed so much. It was quite different than the Early Woodland pottery. Middle Woodland groups started to settle in different areas in the state. The temper (or prehistoric glue) that they used in making their pottery was made up from what they could find nearby, and they used a wider variety of materials than the Early Woodland people. Near the Chesapeake Bay, ground-up quartz and shell were used. In some areas, sand and rocks were used. In other areas, limestone was used. The Middle Woodland people, just like those before them, took these materials, and mixed it with the clay, which provided the ''glue'' effect when a pot or bowl made from the mixture was fired.

bone awl

The tool kit of the Middle Woodland people was much the same as the Early Woodland period. For instance, projectile points were stemmed and notched, just like before. Some bone tools have also been found on Middle Woodland sites like **awls,** used for punching holes in leather and other animal skins.

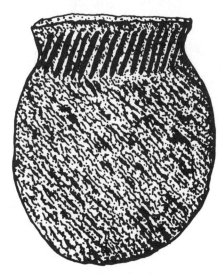

A cordmarked pot

Pottery was made by the coiling method, but a greater variety of materials were being used for tempering. Some materials found locally like shell, limestone, quartz and sand were ground up for the temper.

Middle Woodland camps were close to food and water (no surprises there!), along streams, rivers and marshes. There, the Middle Woodland people ate many different types of food. They hunted deer, turkey, water birds, and gathered berries, nuts and seeds.

turkey

They ate shellfish like oysters and clams. They also ate nuts and plants. Archaeologists have found nut shells and seeds on these sites because they have been preserved.

Houses were much like other times, but they may have been lived in for longer periods of time. Larger groups of many families may have gathered together during summers to enjoy "shellfish banquets," and catch fish which travelled up the rivers during different seasons. However, horticulture (planting) was still very important to the Middle Woodland people. They probably enjoyed many types of plants and vegetables with meals. As you can imagine, the lifestyle of these people was changing as they learned new ways of doing things.

Late Woodland People

The Late Woodland period lasted from A.D. 1000 until A.D. 1600, up until the time of contact with the European settlers who came to America. You have seen the changes that have taken place during the Woodland period. Now you are probably wondering how the Late Woodland people were different from the Early and Middle Woodland people. Well, they had learned from their ancestors, and their lifestyles changed even more as time went by. Archaeologists know more about the Late Woodland period than any other time, because there are so many well-preserved Late Woodland sites in Maryland. Late Woodland people left many artifacts behind—so many that we can learn about them. Archaeologists have excavated Late Woodland sites which are much larger than other sites. This is because Late

Woodland people farmed much larger plots of land to provide more food to feed their growing families. They planted corn, beans and squash, as well as other plants. They relied less on hunting and gathering of wild plants. We know this because archaeologists have found many seeds on Late Woodland sites, as preservation was better.

During this period, people tended to settle down to live in one place for a much longer time. They no longer needed rockshelters and caves. Instead, rockshelters and caves were used for overnight camps when they hunted. They knew how to build bigger and stronger houses from saplings, bark and branches. They didn't need to move around as much because they grew much of their food.

The Late Woodland people lived in **villages** of about 10 to 30 houses.

The houses were placed in a large circle with the doors facing toward a central **plaza.** The plaza was a level open piece of ground that was kept very clean. Some archaeologists think the plaza was used for dancing or ceremonies. There are many postmolds found on Late Woodland village sites. These show what the houses were shaped like and in what places they were built. People lived in family groups, with many families making up a village.

The Late Woodland people chose other spots for their sites. Can you guess why? Hint: They were now farmers. Answer: They chose places with rich soil for growing crops. They also chose sites near rivers and on level hill-

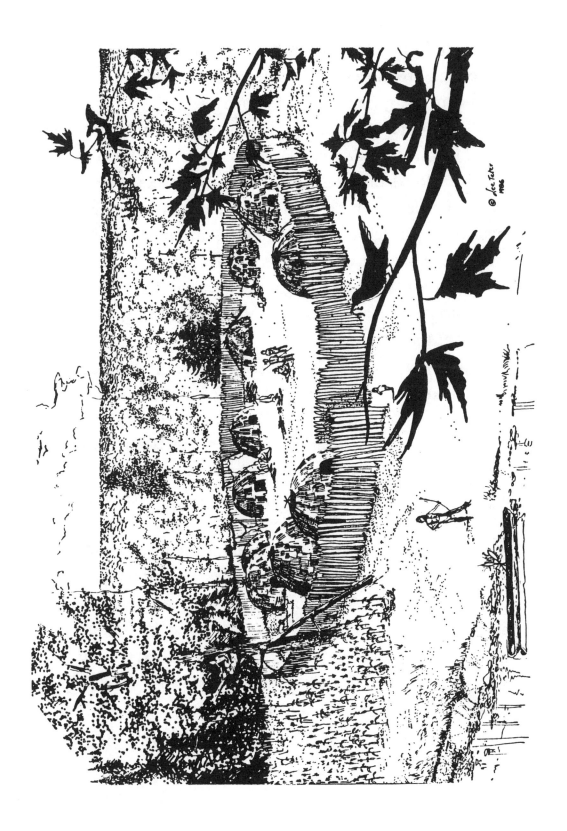

81

tops near freshwater springs and steams. They usually chose high ground next to rivers so they would not be flooded in the spring rain (very smart!).

Villages were all over Maryland, but they didn't always look the same. As you know, the land near the bay and rivers looks different than it does in the mountains. So the people who lived in different parts of Maryland made their villages and pottery a little different too. As these villages grew, the people in them did not have much contact with their neighbors because they didn't really need to. They had just about everything they needed at their own village.

As people got used to living in one place, they hunted the animals close by and used available material for making their stone tools. They used different types of tempering in their pottery, grinding it up from local rocks and shells. Each village decorated their pottery a little different too. Sometimes a group of villages close to each other shared the same pottery-making technology. People who lived in the mountains used freshwater mussel shells (a type of clam) and limestone for tempering in their pottery. The people who lived near the Chesapeake Bay used crushed oyster shells and ground-up quartz or sand for their pottery. Some even used ground up chert. Pots were now shaped like rounded bags. Many were cordmarked and had decorated rims and edges. Some were made into bowls in different sizes. Some even had small handles. Archaeologists have

  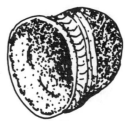

named pottery found in different places in Maryland. The names (called **types**) came from the places where the pottery was found first. When new sites are excavated, the pottery found on that site will be compared with those types already named. If it is similar to one already named, it will be given that name. Otherwise, it will be given a new name.

One important change in Late Woodland times is that a new way of hunting was developed. This was with the **bow and arrow.** The bow and arrow were good for hunting the smaller animals. The **arrowpoint,** or **arrowhead,** as some people like to call them, became much smaller. It was made in the shape of a small triangle.

Small
triangular
point on
an arrow

This type of arrowpoint can be
found all over Maryland, made out
of the available local materials.

As mentioned before, by the material used to temper
pottery and make arrowpoints, people used what was
close by. They no longer went long distances for
material.

The types of animals hunted by the Late Woodland
people in the mountains, meadows and woods of Mary-

Bone
fish hook

land were much the same as those living
in the state today, such as racoons,
squirrels and rabbits. Fish were caught
in fishwiers. Nets were also used. Fish
hooks made of bone have even been
found by archaeologists!

These were all additions to a tool kit that had grown
since Paleo-Indian times. Of course, axes, adzes and
celts were used frequently for building houses.

Other things were happening now that show that
people were thinking of how they looked. Beads were
worn, made out of animal and bird bones and shells
from the ocean. Some unusual necklaces or pendants

84

were made from carving oyster shell or mussel shell into disk shapes. Necklaces were also made from bear and dog teeth which had been drilled and strung. Some archaeologists think bone beads were used to decorate garments.

Smoking was a popular pasttime. Many clay pipes have been found on sites. Some are finely decorated which means their owners must have been very fond of these objects.

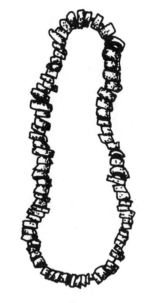

Shell necklace

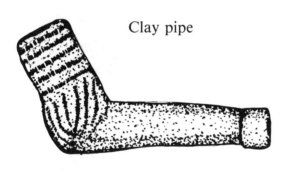

Clay pipe

Since life was a little easier now, there was free time for other activities besides hunting and farming. Some artifacts found on sites tell archaeologists that some things were done for fun. Children may have learned to make pottery with their parents. Like your favorite possessions, these children, like all children, had toy pots to play with. They may have even made them with leftover scraps of clay from making the cooking pots. They also played a game called the **cup and pin**

game. A small cup was made from the toe bone of a deer or elk. After a hole had been drilled into the bone, a string was attached to it with a "pin" (usually a pebble, ball of clay or bone) attached to the other end of the string. The object of the game was to get the pin into the cup without touching the pin! This was a lot of fun for the children. Remember, there were no Saturday morning cartoons! Children helped with the chores in the village and learned what their parents taught them.

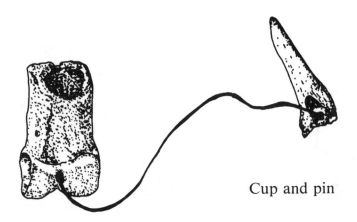

Cup and pin

Adults also played games too. There have been many stones found on sites which have been carved into **disks.**

These are called **discoidals** by the archaeologists. They were used as pieces for a game. Imagine carving a stone into a disk for a gamepiece!

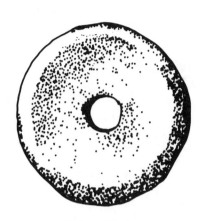

Discoidal

As time went by, some Late Woodland people built large fences around their villages. These fences are called **palisades.** These palisades protected the village. Some archaeologists think that palisades were built to protect the village from other people. They may be right. But some other archaeologists think that the palisades were to protect people from animals and bad weather. In any case, the Late Woodland farmers were living in Maryland at the time the first settlers arrived in Maryland. AND THE REST IS **HISTORY!**

The story does not end with the prehistoric people of Maryland. You will go on to learn about the historic period later. There are some more activities for you to do before you are finished with this unit.

VOCABULARY

Awl   A sharp pointed tool, made from bone, used for punching holes in hides.

Cordmarks   The impressions left on the surface of a pot from a cord wrapped paddle.

Discoidal   A carved round, flat stone that is used as a piece in a game.

Gorget   A stone ground into a square or rectangle for wearing as a pendant around one's neck.

Horticulture   A simple type of farming.

Palisade   A tall wall or fence surrounding a village.

Pendant   A necklace.

Plaza   The central part of a village where people gather for ceremonies.

Temper   Ground up rocks or shell used in the clay to make pots. It helps the clay stick together.

Type   How items in a group are placed in categories. There are types of arrowheads and pottery.

ACTIVITY
TIME CHART

On the next page is a "time chart" which you may use as a "map" of the past. This can be removed from your booklet so you can hang it up in your room. YOU can be the artist for this chart. As you can see, there are blank spaces next to each time period. In each blank space, draw an artifact that you think tells the most about each time period. When you look at your time chart, you will be able to remember your lesson about THE FIRST PEOPLE OF MARYLAND.

MARYLAND'S PAST

Late	A.D 1000 to A.D.1600	**Woodland** **Farmer**	
Middle	500 B.C. to A.D 1000		
Early	1000 B.C. to 500 B.C.		
	8000 B.C. to 1000 B.C.	**Archaic Hunter** **and Gatherer**	
	10000 B.C. to 8000 B.C.	**Paleo - Indian**	

MAP ACTIVITY

Connect the postmolds on the site map below. Can you tell where the houses are? Where the cooking fires were? Where the palisade was? Can you draw a picture of where this village may have been located?

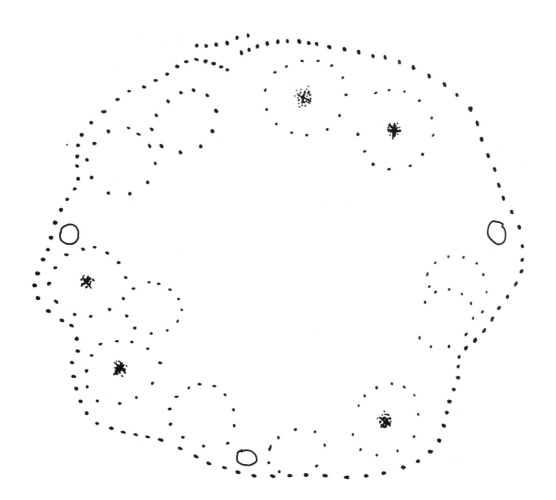

ACTIVITIES
FILL IN THE BLANKS

You have learned about the Paleo-Indians, the Archaic hunters and gatherers, and the Woodland farmers. Read the following statements. Then place in the blank space the time that those things happened. Use **P** for Paleo-Indian, **A** for Archaic hunter and gatherer, or **W** for Woodland farmer. You may use more than one letter.

Example: __A__ Steatite bowls.

1. _____ Tool kit included axes, adzes, triangular points and pottery.

2. _____ Made beautiful fluted spearpoints.

3. _____ Hunted animals and gathered nuts, berries, shellfish and plants with their neighbors.

4. _____ Were greatly influenced by the Wisconsin glacier.

5. _____ Children played the cup and pin game.

6. _____ Lived in villages.

7. _____ Came across the Beringia land bridge.

8. _____ Used steatite bowls and the atlatl.

9. _____ Hunted the mastodon.

10. _____ Wore pendants and smoked pipes.

MAZE GAME

Get the Woodland farmer back to his village after his hunting trip.

CROSSWORD PUZZLE

DOWN

1. A piece of pot or bowl.
3. Ground up rocks or shell used in pottery making.
5. Means "stone."
6. Late Woodland hunter's tools.
8. Finely made Paleo-Indian tool.
9. Slab or bowl which holds nuts or seeds for grinding.
11. Shape of Late Woodland arrowpoints.
12. Projectile_____.
16. Impressions made in pots from a cordwrapped paddle.
19. Woodland _____.
20. Used for smoking.
22. Favorite Paleo-Indian shelter.
23. Handle to a pot.
24. Land Bridge.
25. Center of village.
29. Grassland.

ACROSS

2. Simple farming.
4. Late Woodland farmers lived here.
7. Archaic hunter's tool.
10. Ground stone tool used for woodworking.
13. Late Woodland crop.
14. Cup and _____ game.
15. Circular stains made by decayed posts.
17. Archaic hunters and _____.
18. Means "ancient."
21. Fishwier.
26. Squares which divide a site for excavation.
27. A place where humans were.
28. Tells where all the features and postmolds are on a site.

ACTIVITIES

1. Using your own modelling clay, make a pot using the coiling method. You can use the drawing on page 70 to help you.

2. Make your own cup and pin game using a styrofoam cup, a piece of string (about 4 inches long), and a small piece of your modelling clay. First, punch a small hole in the bottom of the cup. Next, thread one end of the string into the cup and tie a knot at the end inside the cup. Make the knot big enough so it will not pass through the hole in the cup. Then, shape a small ball of clay (about the size of a marble) around the other end of the string. Remember, the object of the game is to get the ball into the cup without touching the ball. Just use one hand with this game! (You may want to have an adult help you make this game.)

APPENDICES

CHAPTERS OF THE
ARCHAEOLOGICAL SOCIETY OF MARYLAND

The following people may be contacted for information about meetings of the archaeological societies:

ANNE ARUNDEL COUNTY: Richard R. Johnson, 5901 Joe Road, Deale, Maryland 20751. Phone: 301-867-0597.

CENTRAL: Norma A.B. Wagner, 3505 Gibbons Avenue, Baltimore, Maryland 21214. Phone: 301-426-0840.

HARFORD COUNTY: Paul Cresthull, 721 Hookers Mill Road, Abingdon, Maryland 21009. Phone: 301-676-7828.

LOWER DELMARVA: Ethel R. Eaton, R.D. 2, Box 174A, Parsonsburg, Maryland 21849. Phone: 301-546-5214.

MID-SHORE: Jaqueline Mullikin, Route 3, Box 457, Easton, Maryland 21601. Phone: 301-822-7820.

NORTHEASTERN: George Reynolds, P.O. Box 3, Elkton, Maryland 21921. Phone: 301-398-6659.

SOUTHERN: Paula Mask, 820 Pat Lane, Huntingtown, Maryland 20639.

UPPER PATUXENT ARCHAEOLOGY GROUP: M. Lee Preston, 1262 Bright Bay Way, Ellicott City, Maryland 21043.

WESTERN MARYLAND ARCHAEOLOGICAL SOCIETY: Victor Smith, Route 1, Box 168, Sharpsburg, Maryland 21782. Phone: 301-432-5972.

ANSWERS TO GAMES
AND ACTIVITIES

WORD GAME
(From Page 25)

Circle the correct answer.

1. Archaeologists "read" prehistoric sites by looking
   at the:
   A. Indian's diary
   B. Road map
   C. Artifacts and features
   D. Rocks

2. Prehistoric man liked to live close to:
   A. Food and water
   B. Fast food restaurants
   C. Golf courses
   D. Home

3. The time before things were written down is called:
   A. History
   B. Prehistory
   C. Confusing
   D. Unknown

4. Archaeologists study an archaeological site by care-
   fully digging layers of earth. This is called:
   A. Science
   B. Work
   C. Mapping
   D. Excavation

5. Any object that people have made or modified is called an:
    A. Oracle
    (B.) Artifact
    C. Artichoke
    D. Tent pole

6. The scientific study of the remains of past human life is done by:
    A. Magicians
    B. Chemists
    (C.) Archaeologists
    D. Musicians

7. When archaeologists divide a site into equal sized squares for excavation, it is then called a:
    A. DigCheck
    B. Checkerboard
    (C.) Grid
    D. Mess

8. When Indians dug holes for storage, burials, fire pits and post holes, archaeologists find them later and call them:
    A. Stonebins
    B. Cradlemounds
    (C.) Features
    D. Ropeyarns

9. When archaeologists sift soil to gather artifacts, this is called:
    A. Digging
    (B.) Screening
    C. Mapping
    D. Designing

10. When archaeologists dig small holes to find out where a site is and to decide how important the artifacts are, these holes are called:
    A. Fire pits
    B. Snakey pits
    C. Test pits
    D. Arm pits

11. Any place that has remains of past human activity is called a:
    A. Cave dig
    B. Post hole
    C. Site
    D. Jammin' stance

12. When an archaeologist writes down all the facts about an excavation into a notebook, they are called:
    A. Fairy tales
    B. Dissertation
    C. Field notes
    D. Journals

13. When an archaeologist talks about what prehistoric people were doing on a site, this is called:
    A. Mind reading
    B. Interpretation
    C. Interlogging
    D. Interstellar navigation

WORD FIND
(From Page 28)

Find the following word in the diagram below, and draw a line in the crossword for each word that you find.

archaeologist	grid	trowel
shovel	field notes	features
survey	interpret	test pit
screening	map	prehistory
excavation	postmold	artifact
plowzone	preservation	subsoil
site		

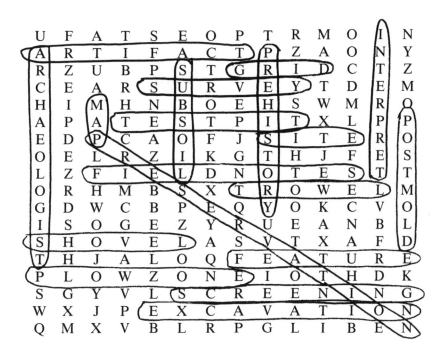

VOCABULARY ACTIVITIES
(From Page 45)

Can you match the following words?

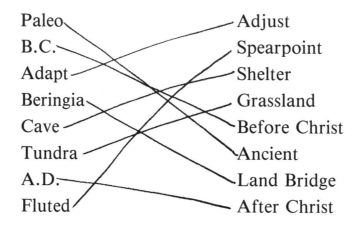

Paleo — Ancient
B.C. — Before Christ
Adapt — Adjust
Beringia — Land Bridge
Cave — Shelter
Tundra — Grassland
A.D. — After Christ
Fluted — Spearpoint

SCRAMBLED WORDS

dfutel rpostapeni	fluted spearpoint
adnl rbiegde	land bridge
ahsmetomrn	hammerstone
aciburo	caribou
srkhetlocer	rockshelter
fekla	flake
tafricta	artifact
gicelar	glacier

ACTIVITIES
FILL IN THE BLANKS
(From Page 92)

You have learned about the Paleo-Indians, the Archaic hunters and gatherers, and the Woodland farmers. Read the following statements. Then place in the blank space the time that those things happened. Use **P** for Paleo-Indian, **A** for Archaic hunter and gatherer, or **W** for Woodland farmer. You may use more than one letter.

Example: __A__ Steatite bowls.

1. __W__ Tool kit included axes, adzes, triangular points and pottery.

2. __P__ Made beautiful fluted spearpoints.

3. __A,W__ Hunted animals and gathered nuts, berries, shellfish and plants with their neighbors.

4. __P__ Were greatly influenced by the Wisconsin glacier.

5. __W__ Children played the cup and pin game.

6. __W__ Lived in villages.

7. __P__ Came across the Beringia land bridge.

8. __A__ Used steatite bowls and the atlatl.

9. __P__ Hunted the mastodon.

10. __W__ Wore pendants and smoked pipes.

CROSSWORD PUZZLE
(From Page 95)

ADDITIONAL RESOURCES FOR TEACHERS

Adams, George, and Patricia Hall
1983   Planning and Conducting Successful Seminars and Workshops. *American Association for State and Local History Technical Leaflet,* 146.

Bostick, Linda
1985   My Digs in Majorca. *Science Teacher,* 52(7):35.

Danes, Lois M.
1981   Archaeology in the Classroom. *Science and Children,* 19(1):40-41.

Fladung, Edmund B., and Richard Stearns
1950   Our Maryland Indians. *Maryland Naturalist,* 20(3): 61-64.

Holm, Karen
1984   Can You Dig It? *Science Teacher,* 51(4):48-49.

Hotchkiss, Ron
1981   A New Use for Old Garbage. *History and Social Science Teacher,* 17(1):44-45.

Jaus, Harold H.
1975   Digging Science. *Science and Children,* 13(1):30-31.

Kraft, Herbert, and John T. Kraft
1985   Resource and Activities Supplement for the Indians of Lenapehoking. *Archaeological Research Center Seton Hall University Press.*

Law, Shirley Payne
1965   Historic Site Interpretation: The Human Approach. American Association for State and Local History Technical Leaflet, 32.

Manakee, Harold R.
1958   *Indians of Early Maryland.* Historical Society of Baltimore.

McNett, Charles, Ann Ferren, and Richard Dent
1983   Final Report American Indian Archaeology in the Middle School: Supplemental Materials for American History Courses. *Potomac River Archaeology Survey, American University, Washington, D.C.*

Morrissett, Irving (editor)

1982   Social Studies in the 1980s. *Alexandria Association for Supervision and Curriculum Development.*

Plants, Robert W.

1984   Projectile Point Classification. *Science and Children,* 21(5):6-9.

Porter, Frank W.

1983   *Maryland Indians Yesterday and Today.* The Maryland Historical Society, Baltimore.

Ruskin, Thelma

1986   *Indians of the Tidewater Country.* Lanham, MD: Maryland Historical Press.

Stone, John R.

1978   Archaeology: Resources for the Classroom. *History and Social Science Teacher,* 14(1):15-20.

Watts, Lou Ellen

1985   They Dig Archaeology. *Science and Children,* 23(1):5-9.

INDEX